50 Mustard Dishes

By: Kelly Johnson

Table of Contents

- Mustard Glazed Chicken
- Mustard Potato Salad
- Honey Mustard Chicken Tenders
- Mustard Pork Chops
- Mustard Deviled Eggs
- Mustard Mac and Cheese
- Mustard Vinaigrette Salad Dressing
- Mustard Grilled Sausages
- Mustard Shrimp Skewers
- Mustard Roasted Brussels Sprouts
- Mustard Slaw
- Mustard Baked Ham
- Mustard Chicken Wings
- Mustard Cabbage Salad
- Mustard-Glazed Salmon
- Mustard and Herb Roasted Potatoes
- Mustard Fried Chicken
- Mustard Dressing for Roasted Vegetables
- Mustard BBQ Ribs
- Mustard-Marinated Steak
- Mustard Pickled Vegetables
- Mustard Gravy for Meatloaf
- Mustard and Honey Glazed Carrots
- Mustard-Stuffed Mushrooms
- Mustard Chicken Salad
- Mustard Pretzel Dip
- Mustard Shrimp Salad
- Mustard and Dill Potato Salad
- Mustard Steak Sandwich
- Mustard and Bacon Potato Skins
- Mustard Roasted Sweet Potatoes
- Mustard-Glazed Tofu
- Mustard Chicken Tacos
- Mustard-Crusted Fish Fillets
- Mustard Hummus

- Mustard Meatball Sub
- Mustard and Tomato Soup
- Mustard Bacon-Wrapped Asparagus
- Mustard Vinaigrette for Green Beans
- Mustard-Marinated Grilled Chicken
- Mustard and Sausage Pasta
- Mustard Baked Ziti
- Mustard Grilled Cheese Sandwich
- Mustard and Onion Relish
- Mustard Egg Salad
- Mustard Glazed Meatballs
- Mustard Roasted Chicken Thighs
- Mustard Coleslaw
- Mustard and Bacon Deviled Eggs
- Mustard-Crusted Roasted Lamb

Mustard Glazed Chicken

Ingredients:

- 4 chicken breasts
- 1/4 cup Dijon mustard
- 2 tablespoons honey
- 1 tablespoon olive oil
- 1 teaspoon garlic powder
- Salt and pepper to taste
- Fresh parsley for garnish

Instructions:

1. Preheat the oven to 375°F (190°C).
2. In a small bowl, whisk together Dijon mustard, honey, olive oil, garlic powder, salt, and pepper.
3. Brush the chicken breasts with the mustard glaze and place them on a baking sheet.
4. Bake for 25-30 minutes, or until the chicken reaches an internal temperature of 165°F (74°C).
5. Garnish with fresh parsley and serve with your favorite side dishes.

Mustard Potato Salad

Ingredients:

- 2 lbs baby potatoes, boiled and cubed
- 1/4 cup Dijon mustard
- 2 tablespoons mayonnaise
- 1 tablespoon apple cider vinegar
- 1 tablespoon olive oil
- 1/4 teaspoon paprika
- Salt and pepper to taste
- 1/4 cup chopped fresh parsley

Instructions:

1. In a large bowl, combine the boiled and cubed potatoes.
2. In a separate bowl, whisk together Dijon mustard, mayonnaise, apple cider vinegar, olive oil, paprika, salt, and pepper.
3. Pour the mustard dressing over the potatoes and toss gently to coat.
4. Garnish with fresh parsley and serve chilled.

Honey Mustard Chicken Tenders

Ingredients:

- 1 lb chicken tenders
- 1/4 cup Dijon mustard
- 2 tablespoons honey
- 1 tablespoon olive oil
- 1/2 teaspoon garlic powder
- Salt and pepper to taste

Instructions:

1. Preheat the oven to 400°F (200°C).
2. In a small bowl, whisk together Dijon mustard, honey, olive oil, garlic powder, salt, and pepper.
3. Coat the chicken tenders with the mustard glaze and arrange them on a baking sheet.
4. Bake for 15-20 minutes, or until the chicken is cooked through and crispy on the edges.
5. Serve with your favorite dipping sauce.

Mustard Pork Chops

Ingredients:

- 4 pork chops
- 1/4 cup Dijon mustard
- 1 tablespoon honey
- 1 tablespoon olive oil
- 1 teaspoon thyme
- Salt and pepper to taste

Instructions:

1. Preheat the oven to 375°F (190°C).
2. In a small bowl, whisk together Dijon mustard, honey, olive oil, thyme, salt, and pepper.
3. Brush the mustard mixture over the pork chops and place them on a baking sheet.
4. Bake for 25-30 minutes, or until the pork reaches an internal temperature of 145°F (63°C).
5. Let the pork chops rest for 5 minutes before serving.

Mustard Deviled Eggs

Ingredients:

- 6 hard-boiled eggs, peeled
- 2 tablespoons Dijon mustard
- 1/4 cup mayonnaise
- 1 tablespoon vinegar
- 1 teaspoon paprika
- Salt and pepper to taste
- Fresh chives for garnish

Instructions:

1. Slice the hard-boiled eggs in half and remove the yolks.
2. In a bowl, mash the yolks and mix with Dijon mustard, mayonnaise, vinegar, salt, and pepper.
3. Spoon or pipe the mixture back into the egg whites.
4. Sprinkle with paprika and garnish with fresh chives.
5. Serve chilled.

Mustard Mac and Cheese

Ingredients:

- 1 lb elbow macaroni, cooked
- 2 tablespoons butter
- 2 tablespoons flour
- 2 cups milk
- 1 1/2 cups shredded cheddar cheese
- 2 tablespoons Dijon mustard
- Salt and pepper to taste

Instructions:

1. In a large saucepan, melt butter over medium heat. Stir in the flour and cook for 1-2 minutes.
2. Slowly whisk in the milk and cook until the sauce thickens, about 5-7 minutes.
3. Stir in the shredded cheddar cheese and Dijon mustard. Continue stirring until the cheese is melted and smooth.
4. Season with salt and pepper, then toss with the cooked macaroni.
5. Serve hot for a creamy, tangy twist on classic mac and cheese.

Mustard Vinaigrette Salad Dressing

Ingredients:

- 3 tablespoons Dijon mustard
- 1/4 cup white wine vinegar
- 1/2 cup olive oil
- 1 teaspoon honey
- Salt and pepper to taste

Instructions:

1. In a small bowl or jar, whisk together Dijon mustard, white wine vinegar, honey, salt, and pepper.
2. Gradually whisk in the olive oil until the dressing is emulsified and smooth.
3. Drizzle over your favorite salad and toss to coat.

Mustard Grilled Sausages

Ingredients:

- 4 sausages of your choice
- 1/4 cup Dijon mustard
- 1 tablespoon honey
- 1 tablespoon apple cider vinegar
- Salt and pepper to taste

Instructions:

1. Preheat the grill to medium heat.
2. In a small bowl, whisk together Dijon mustard, honey, apple cider vinegar, salt, and pepper.
3. Grill the sausages for 8-10 minutes, turning occasionally until they are cooked through and have nice grill marks.
4. Brush the mustard glaze onto the sausages during the last few minutes of grilling.
5. Serve hot with your favorite sides.

Mustard Shrimp Skewers

Ingredients:

- 1 lb large shrimp, peeled and deveined
- 1/4 cup Dijon mustard
- 2 tablespoons olive oil
- 1 tablespoon lemon juice
- 1 teaspoon garlic powder
- Salt and pepper to taste

Instructions:

1. Preheat the grill to medium heat.
2. In a bowl, whisk together Dijon mustard, olive oil, lemon juice, garlic powder, salt, and pepper.
3. Toss the shrimp in the mustard marinade and thread them onto skewers.
4. Grill the shrimp for 2-3 minutes per side, or until pink and cooked through.
5. Serve hot with a squeeze of lemon juice.

Mustard Roasted Brussels Sprouts

Ingredients:

- 1 lb Brussels sprouts, trimmed and halved
- 2 tablespoons Dijon mustard
- 2 tablespoons olive oil
- 1 tablespoon honey
- Salt and pepper to taste
- 1/4 teaspoon garlic powder

Instructions:

1. Preheat the oven to 400°F (200°C).
2. In a bowl, whisk together Dijon mustard, olive oil, honey, salt, pepper, and garlic powder.
3. Toss the halved Brussels sprouts in the mustard mixture and spread them on a baking sheet.
4. Roast for 20-25 minutes, or until crispy and caramelized.
5. Serve as a tasty side dish.

Mustard Slaw

Ingredients:

- 4 cups shredded cabbage
- 1/2 cup shredded carrots
- 1/4 cup Dijon mustard
- 1/4 cup mayonnaise
- 1 tablespoon apple cider vinegar
- 1 tablespoon honey
- Salt and pepper to taste

Instructions:

1. In a large bowl, combine the shredded cabbage and carrots.
2. In a separate bowl, whisk together Dijon mustard, mayonnaise, apple cider vinegar, honey, salt, and pepper.
3. Pour the dressing over the cabbage mixture and toss to coat evenly.
4. Chill for at least 30 minutes before serving to allow flavors to meld.

Mustard Baked Ham

Ingredients:

- 1 boneless ham (about 5 lbs)
- 1/4 cup Dijon mustard
- 1/4 cup brown sugar
- 1 tablespoon apple cider vinegar
- 1/4 teaspoon ground cloves
- 1/4 teaspoon cinnamon
- Salt and pepper to taste

Instructions:

1. Preheat the oven to 350°F (175°C).
2. Place the ham in a roasting pan and score the top with shallow cuts in a diamond pattern.
3. In a small bowl, mix Dijon mustard, brown sugar, apple cider vinegar, ground cloves, cinnamon, salt, and pepper.
4. Brush the mustard glaze generously over the ham.
5. Bake for 1.5 to 2 hours, basting with the glaze every 30 minutes, until the ham reaches an internal temperature of 140°F (60°C).
6. Let rest before slicing and serving.

Mustard Chicken Wings

Ingredients:

- 10 chicken wings
- 2 tablespoons Dijon mustard
- 1 tablespoon honey
- 1 tablespoon olive oil
- 1/2 teaspoon garlic powder
- Salt and pepper to taste

Instructions:

1. Preheat the oven to 400°F (200°C).
2. In a small bowl, whisk together Dijon mustard, honey, olive oil, garlic powder, salt, and pepper.
3. Toss the chicken wings in the mustard mixture and place them on a baking sheet.
4. Bake for 25-30 minutes, flipping halfway through, until crispy and golden.
5. Serve hot with your favorite dipping sauce.

Mustard Cabbage Salad

Ingredients:

- 4 cups shredded cabbage
- 1/4 cup Dijon mustard
- 2 tablespoons white wine vinegar
- 2 tablespoons olive oil
- 1 tablespoon honey
- Salt and pepper to taste
- 1/4 cup chopped parsley

Instructions:

1. In a large bowl, combine shredded cabbage and chopped parsley.
2. In a separate bowl, whisk together Dijon mustard, white wine vinegar, olive oil, honey, salt, and pepper.
3. Pour the mustard dressing over the cabbage and toss to combine.
4. Chill for 20 minutes before serving.

Mustard-Glazed Salmon

Ingredients:

- 4 salmon fillets
- 2 tablespoons Dijon mustard
- 1 tablespoon honey
- 1 tablespoon lemon juice
- Salt and pepper to taste

Instructions:

1. Preheat the oven to 375°F (190°C).
2. In a small bowl, whisk together Dijon mustard, honey, lemon juice, salt, and pepper.
3. Place the salmon fillets on a baking sheet lined with parchment paper.
4. Brush the mustard glaze over the salmon fillets.
5. Bake for 12-15 minutes, or until the salmon is cooked through.
6. Serve with a side of roasted vegetables.

Mustard and Herb Roasted Potatoes

Ingredients:

- 2 lbs baby potatoes, halved
- 2 tablespoons Dijon mustard
- 1 tablespoon olive oil
- 1 tablespoon fresh rosemary, chopped
- 1 tablespoon fresh thyme, chopped
- Salt and pepper to taste

Instructions:

1. Preheat the oven to 400°F (200°C).
2. In a bowl, whisk together Dijon mustard, olive oil, fresh rosemary, fresh thyme, salt, and pepper.
3. Toss the halved potatoes in the mustard mixture and spread them in a single layer on a baking sheet.
4. Roast for 25-30 minutes, or until golden and crispy on the outside.
5. Serve hot as a flavorful side dish.

Mustard Fried Chicken

Ingredients:

- 4 chicken breasts or thighs
- 1/4 cup Dijon mustard
- 1/4 cup buttermilk
- 1 cup flour
- 1 teaspoon paprika
- 1 teaspoon garlic powder
- Salt and pepper to taste
- Vegetable oil for frying

Instructions:

1. In a bowl, combine Dijon mustard and buttermilk. Add the chicken pieces and marinate for at least 1 hour.
2. In another bowl, mix together flour, paprika, garlic powder, salt, and pepper.
3. Dredge the marinated chicken in the flour mixture.
4. Heat oil in a skillet over medium-high heat. Fry the chicken for 6-8 minutes per side, or until golden and crispy.
5. Drain on paper towels and serve.

Mustard Dressing for Roasted Vegetables

Ingredients:

- 2 tablespoons Dijon mustard
- 2 tablespoons olive oil
- 1 tablespoon lemon juice
- 1 teaspoon honey
- Salt and pepper to taste

Instructions:

1. In a small bowl, whisk together Dijon mustard, olive oil, lemon juice, honey, salt, and pepper.
2. Drizzle the mustard dressing over your favorite roasted vegetables, such as Brussels sprouts, carrots, or sweet potatoes.
3. Toss to coat and serve warm.

Mustard BBQ Ribs

Ingredients:

- 2 racks of baby back ribs
- 1/4 cup Dijon mustard
- 1/2 cup BBQ sauce
- 2 tablespoons honey
- 1 tablespoon apple cider vinegar
- Salt and pepper to taste

Instructions:

1. Preheat your grill to medium-high heat.
2. Rub the ribs with Dijon mustard and season with salt and pepper.
3. In a bowl, mix BBQ sauce, honey, and apple cider vinegar.
4. Grill the ribs for about 2 hours, turning occasionally and basting with the mustard BBQ glaze.
5. Serve hot with extra BBQ sauce on the side.

Mustard-Marinated Steak

Ingredients:

- 4 steaks (your choice of cut)
- 3 tablespoons Dijon mustard
- 2 tablespoons olive oil
- 1 tablespoon balsamic vinegar
- 1 teaspoon garlic powder
- Salt and pepper to taste

Instructions:

1. In a bowl, whisk together Dijon mustard, olive oil, balsamic vinegar, garlic powder, salt, and pepper.
2. Coat the steaks with the marinade and refrigerate for at least 1 hour, or overnight for a stronger flavor.
3. Preheat your grill or skillet to medium-high heat.
4. Cook the steaks to your desired level of doneness, about 4-6 minutes per side.
5. Let the steaks rest before serving with your favorite side dishes.

Mustard Pickled Vegetables

Ingredients:

- 2 cups mixed vegetables (carrots, cauliflower, cucumbers)
- 1/2 cup white vinegar
- 1/4 cup Dijon mustard
- 1/2 cup water
- 1 tablespoon honey
- 1/4 teaspoon turmeric
- 1/4 teaspoon mustard seeds
- Salt to taste

Instructions:

1. In a saucepan, combine vinegar, Dijon mustard, water, honey, turmeric, mustard seeds, and salt. Bring to a boil, then simmer for 5 minutes.
2. Place the mixed vegetables in a jar or container.
3. Pour the hot mustard brine over the vegetables, ensuring they are fully submerged.
4. Allow to cool, then refrigerate for at least 24 hours before serving as a tangy, crunchy side.

Mustard Gravy for Meatloaf

Ingredients:

- 1/2 cup Dijon mustard
- 1 cup beef broth
- 2 tablespoons flour
- 1 tablespoon butter
- Salt and pepper to taste

Instructions:

1. In a saucepan, melt the butter over medium heat. Add flour and whisk to form a roux.
2. Gradually add beef broth, whisking continuously until smooth.
3. Stir in Dijon mustard, salt, and pepper. Cook for 2-3 minutes until thickened.
4. Pour over meatloaf slices and serve.

Mustard and Honey Glazed Carrots

Ingredients:

- 4 cups baby carrots
- 2 tablespoons Dijon mustard
- 1 tablespoon honey
- 1 tablespoon olive oil
- Salt and pepper to taste

Instructions:

1. Preheat the oven to 375°F (190°C).
2. In a bowl, whisk together Dijon mustard, honey, olive oil, salt, and pepper.
3. Toss the carrots in the mustard glaze and spread them on a baking sheet.
4. Roast for 20-25 minutes, or until tender and caramelized, stirring halfway through.

Mustard-Stuffed Mushrooms

Ingredients:

- 12 large mushroom caps
- 2 tablespoons Dijon mustard
- 4 oz cream cheese, softened
- 1/4 cup grated Parmesan cheese
- 1 tablespoon fresh parsley, chopped
- Salt and pepper to taste

Instructions:

1. Preheat your oven to 375°F (190°C).
2. In a bowl, mix Dijon mustard, cream cheese, Parmesan, parsley, salt, and pepper.
3. Stuff the mushroom caps with the mustard mixture and place them on a baking sheet.
4. Bake for 15-20 minutes, or until the mushrooms are tender and the stuffing is golden.

Mustard Chicken Salad

Ingredients:

- 2 cups cooked chicken, shredded
- 1/4 cup Dijon mustard
- 1/4 cup mayonnaise
- 1 tablespoon lemon juice
- 1 tablespoon fresh dill, chopped
- Salt and pepper to taste

Instructions:

1. In a bowl, combine Dijon mustard, mayonnaise, lemon juice, dill, salt, and pepper.
2. Toss with the shredded chicken until evenly coated.
3. Serve as a sandwich or over a bed of greens.

Mustard Pretzel Dip

Ingredients:

- 1/2 cup Dijon mustard
- 1/4 cup cream cheese, softened
- 1 tablespoon honey
- 1 tablespoon white vinegar
- 1/2 teaspoon garlic powder

Instructions:

1. In a bowl, combine Dijon mustard, cream cheese, honey, white vinegar, and garlic powder.
2. Mix until smooth and creamy.
3. Serve with pretzels for a tangy and creamy dip.

Mustard Shrimp Salad

Ingredients:

- 1 lb cooked shrimp, peeled and deveined
- 1/4 cup Dijon mustard
- 1 tablespoon mayonnaise
- 1 tablespoon lemon juice
- 1/4 cup celery, finely chopped
- 1/4 cup red onion, finely chopped
- Salt and pepper to taste

Instructions:

1. In a bowl, mix Dijon mustard, mayonnaise, lemon juice, celery, red onion, salt, and pepper.
2. Add the cooked shrimp and toss to coat.
3. Serve the shrimp salad on lettuce leaves or as a sandwich filling.

Mustard and Dill Potato Salad

Ingredients:

- 6 medium potatoes, boiled and diced
- 1/4 cup Dijon mustard
- 1/4 cup sour cream
- 2 tablespoons mayonnaise
- 2 tablespoons fresh dill, chopped
- 1 tablespoon white vinegar
- Salt and pepper to taste

Instructions:

1. In a bowl, combine Dijon mustard, sour cream, mayonnaise, dill, vinegar, salt, and pepper.
2. Toss the boiled and diced potatoes in the dressing mixture until evenly coated.
3. Chill in the refrigerator for at least 1 hour before serving for the best flavor.

Mustard Steak Sandwich

Ingredients:

- 1 lb ribeye or flank steak
- 2 tablespoons Dijon mustard
- 1 tablespoon olive oil
- 1 teaspoon garlic powder
- Salt and pepper to taste
- 4 sandwich rolls
- 1/4 cup arugula or spinach
- 1/2 onion, sliced and caramelized (optional)

Instructions:

1. Preheat your grill or skillet over medium-high heat.
2. Rub the steak with Dijon mustard, olive oil, garlic powder, salt, and pepper.
3. Grill the steak for about 5-7 minutes per side (for medium rare), then rest for 5 minutes.
4. Slice the steak thinly and assemble the sandwich with arugula, caramelized onions (if desired), and the steak on sandwich rolls.

Mustard and Bacon Potato Skins

Ingredients:

- 4 large russet potatoes
- 1/4 cup Dijon mustard
- 4 slices bacon, cooked and crumbled
- 1/2 cup shredded cheddar cheese
- 1/4 cup sour cream
- Salt and pepper to taste
- Chives, chopped, for garnish

Instructions:

1. Preheat the oven to 400°F (200°C).
2. Bake the potatoes for 45 minutes or until tender. Once cooled slightly, cut the potatoes in half and scoop out the insides.
3. Brush the potato skins with Dijon mustard and season with salt and pepper.
4. Fill the potato skins with crumbled bacon, shredded cheese, and a dollop of sour cream.
5. Bake for another 10 minutes until the cheese is melted. Garnish with chopped chives and serve.

Mustard Roasted Sweet Potatoes

Ingredients:

- 4 medium sweet potatoes, peeled and diced
- 2 tablespoons Dijon mustard
- 1 tablespoon olive oil
- 1 teaspoon maple syrup
- 1 teaspoon ground cumin
- Salt and pepper to taste

Instructions:

1. Preheat the oven to 400°F (200°C).
2. In a bowl, whisk together Dijon mustard, olive oil, maple syrup, cumin, salt, and pepper.
3. Toss the diced sweet potatoes in the mustard mixture and spread them on a baking sheet.
4. Roast for 25-30 minutes, stirring halfway through, until the sweet potatoes are tender and caramelized.

Mustard-Glazed Tofu

Ingredients:

- 1 block firm tofu, drained and pressed
- 3 tablespoons Dijon mustard
- 1 tablespoon soy sauce
- 1 tablespoon maple syrup
- 1 teaspoon garlic powder
- Salt and pepper to taste

Instructions:

1. Preheat your oven to 375°F (190°C).
2. Slice the tofu into 1-inch thick slabs and arrange on a baking sheet.
3. In a bowl, whisk together Dijon mustard, soy sauce, maple syrup, garlic powder, salt, and pepper.
4. Brush the tofu with the mustard glaze and bake for 25-30 minutes, flipping halfway, until crispy and golden.

Mustard Chicken Tacos

Ingredients:

- 1 lb chicken breast, cooked and shredded
- 2 tablespoons Dijon mustard
- 1 tablespoon lime juice
- 1 teaspoon chili powder
- Salt and pepper to taste
- Small tortillas
- Toppings: shredded lettuce, diced tomatoes, avocado, cilantro

Instructions:

1. In a bowl, mix Dijon mustard, lime juice, chili powder, salt, and pepper.
2. Toss the shredded chicken in the mustard mixture until fully coated.
3. Heat the tortillas and assemble the tacos with the mustard chicken and desired toppings.

Mustard-Crusted Fish Fillets

Ingredients:

- 4 white fish fillets (cod, tilapia, or haddock)
- 2 tablespoons Dijon mustard
- 1/2 cup panko breadcrumbs
- 2 tablespoons parsley, chopped
- 1 tablespoon olive oil
- Salt and pepper to taste

Instructions:

1. Preheat the oven to 400°F (200°C).
2. Coat each fish fillet with Dijon mustard and season with salt and pepper.
3. In a separate bowl, combine panko breadcrumbs, parsley, and olive oil.
4. Press the mustard-coated fillets into the breadcrumb mixture.
5. Place the fillets on a baking sheet and bake for 12-15 minutes, until golden and crispy.

Mustard Hummus

Ingredients:

- 1 can (15 oz) chickpeas, drained and rinsed
- 2 tablespoons Dijon mustard
- 2 tablespoons tahini
- 1 tablespoon lemon juice
- 1 garlic clove, minced
- 1 tablespoon olive oil
- Salt and pepper to taste

Instructions:

1. In a food processor, combine chickpeas, Dijon mustard, tahini, lemon juice, garlic, olive oil, salt, and pepper.
2. Blend until smooth, adding a little water if needed to achieve desired consistency.
3. Serve with pita chips or fresh vegetables.

Mustard Meatball Sub

Ingredients:

- 1 lb ground beef or turkey
- 1/4 cup breadcrumbs
- 1 egg
- 2 tablespoons Dijon mustard
- 1/2 teaspoon garlic powder
- Salt and pepper to taste
- 4 sub rolls
- 1 cup marinara sauce
- 1/2 cup mozzarella cheese, shredded

Instructions:

1. Preheat the oven to 375°F (190°C).
2. In a bowl, combine ground meat, breadcrumbs, egg, Dijon mustard, garlic powder, salt, and pepper. Form into meatballs.
3. Place the meatballs on a baking sheet and bake for 20-25 minutes, until cooked through.
4. Heat marinara sauce and add the meatballs. Serve on sub rolls, topped with marinara sauce and mozzarella cheese.
5. Optionally, broil for 2-3 minutes to melt the cheese.

Mustard and Tomato Soup

Ingredients:

- 1 can (28 oz) crushed tomatoes
- 1 tablespoon Dijon mustard
- 1/2 cup vegetable broth
- 1/2 cup heavy cream
- 1 tablespoon olive oil
- 1 onion, chopped
- 2 garlic cloves, minced
- 1 teaspoon dried basil
- Salt and pepper to taste

Instructions:

1. Heat olive oil in a pot over medium heat. Add chopped onion and minced garlic, sautéing until softened.
2. Add crushed tomatoes, vegetable broth, Dijon mustard, basil, salt, and pepper. Bring to a simmer and cook for 15 minutes.
3. Stir in heavy cream and adjust seasoning to taste.
4. Use an immersion blender to blend the soup until smooth, or transfer to a blender and blend in batches.
5. Serve hot, garnished with fresh herbs or croutons.

Mustard Bacon-Wrapped Asparagus

Ingredients:

- 12 asparagus spears, trimmed
- 6 slices bacon
- 2 tablespoons Dijon mustard
- 1 tablespoon honey
- Salt and pepper to taste

Instructions:

1. Preheat the oven to 400°F (200°C).
2. In a small bowl, mix Dijon mustard, honey, salt, and pepper.
3. Brush the asparagus with the mustard mixture.
4. Wrap each asparagus spear with a slice of bacon and place on a baking sheet.
5. Roast for 15-20 minutes, or until the bacon is crispy and the asparagus is tender.

Mustard Vinaigrette for Green Beans

Ingredients:

- 2 tablespoons Dijon mustard
- 2 tablespoons white wine vinegar
- 1/4 cup olive oil
- 1 teaspoon honey
- Salt and pepper to taste
- 1 lb fresh green beans, blanched

Instructions:

1. In a small bowl, whisk together Dijon mustard, vinegar, olive oil, honey, salt, and pepper.
2. Toss the blanched green beans in the mustard vinaigrette until well coated.
3. Serve immediately, or refrigerate until ready to serve.

Mustard-Marinated Grilled Chicken

Ingredients:

- 4 chicken breasts
- 3 tablespoons Dijon mustard
- 1 tablespoon olive oil
- 1 tablespoon lemon juice
- 2 garlic cloves, minced
- 1 teaspoon dried thyme
- Salt and pepper to taste

Instructions:

1. In a bowl, whisk together Dijon mustard, olive oil, lemon juice, garlic, thyme, salt, and pepper.
2. Place chicken breasts in a resealable plastic bag and pour the marinade over the chicken. Refrigerate for at least 1 hour, or overnight for more flavor.
3. Preheat the grill to medium-high heat. Grill the chicken for 6-7 minutes per side, or until fully cooked.
4. Serve with your favorite sides.

Mustard and Sausage Pasta

Ingredients:

- 1 lb pasta (penne or rigatoni)
- 2 sausage links, casings removed and crumbled
- 2 tablespoons Dijon mustard
- 1/4 cup cream
- 1/4 cup grated Parmesan cheese
- Salt and pepper to taste
- Fresh parsley, chopped for garnish

Instructions:

1. Cook the pasta according to package directions. Drain and set aside.
2. In a large pan, cook the crumbled sausage over medium heat until browned. Remove excess fat.
3. Add Dijon mustard, cream, and Parmesan to the sausage. Stir to combine and cook for 2-3 minutes.
4. Toss the cooked pasta in the mustard sauce and season with salt and pepper.
5. Garnish with fresh parsley and serve.

Mustard Baked Ziti

Ingredients:

- 1 lb ziti pasta
- 1 tablespoon Dijon mustard
- 1 jar (24 oz) marinara sauce
- 2 cups shredded mozzarella cheese
- 1/2 cup grated Parmesan cheese
- 1/4 cup fresh basil, chopped
- Salt and pepper to taste

Instructions:

1. Preheat the oven to 375°F (190°C).
2. Cook the ziti pasta according to package directions, then drain and set aside.
3. In a large bowl, mix together Dijon mustard, marinara sauce, mozzarella cheese, Parmesan, basil, salt, and pepper.
4. Add the cooked pasta to the sauce mixture and stir to coat.
5. Pour the pasta and sauce mixture into a baking dish and top with extra mozzarella cheese.
6. Bake for 20-25 minutes until the cheese is melted and bubbly. Serve hot.

Mustard Grilled Cheese Sandwich

Ingredients:

- 4 slices bread (your choice)
- 4 slices cheddar cheese
- 2 tablespoons Dijon mustard
- 1 tablespoon butter

Instructions:

1. Heat a skillet over medium heat.
2. Spread Dijon mustard on one side of each slice of bread.
3. Place a slice of cheese between two slices of bread, mustard side facing the cheese.
4. Butter the outside of the sandwich and grill in the skillet until golden brown on both sides and the cheese is melted, about 4-5 minutes per side.
5. Serve with a side of tomato soup for a classic combination.

Mustard and Onion Relish

Ingredients:

- 1 large onion, thinly sliced
- 1/4 cup Dijon mustard
- 1 tablespoon sugar
- 2 tablespoons apple cider vinegar
- 1 tablespoon olive oil
- Salt and pepper to taste

Instructions:

1. Heat olive oil in a pan over medium heat and sauté the onions until soft and caramelized, about 15 minutes.
2. Add Dijon mustard, sugar, apple cider vinegar, salt, and pepper. Stir to combine and simmer for an additional 5-7 minutes.
3. Serve as a topping for burgers, hot dogs, or grilled meats.

Mustard Egg Salad

Ingredients:

- 6 hard-boiled eggs, chopped
- 2 tablespoons Dijon mustard
- 1/4 cup mayonnaise
- 1 tablespoon white wine vinegar
- 1 teaspoon honey
- Salt and pepper to taste
- Fresh chives, chopped for garnish

Instructions:

1. In a bowl, combine the chopped eggs, Dijon mustard, mayonnaise, vinegar, honey, salt, and pepper.
2. Stir until well mixed. Adjust the seasoning if necessary.
3. Garnish with chopped chives and serve chilled, on a bed of greens or as a sandwich filling.

Mustard Glazed Meatballs

Ingredients:

- 1 lb ground beef or turkey
- 1/4 cup Dijon mustard
- 2 tablespoons honey
- 1 tablespoon soy sauce
- 1 teaspoon garlic powder
- 1/2 teaspoon salt
- 1/2 teaspoon pepper
- 1 egg
- 1/4 cup breadcrumbs

Instructions:

1. Preheat the oven to 375°F (190°C). Line a baking sheet with parchment paper.
2. In a bowl, combine the ground meat, Dijon mustard, honey, soy sauce, garlic powder, salt, pepper, egg, and breadcrumbs.
3. Mix until everything is well combined. Roll into 1-inch meatballs and place on the baking sheet.
4. Bake for 20-25 minutes, until the meatballs are cooked through and browned.
5. Serve with additional mustard sauce or drizzle with honey mustard glaze.

Mustard Roasted Chicken Thighs

Ingredients:

- 4 chicken thighs, bone-in, skin-on
- 2 tablespoons Dijon mustard
- 1 tablespoon olive oil
- 1 tablespoon honey
- 1 teaspoon dried thyme
- Salt and pepper to taste
- 1 lemon, sliced

Instructions:

1. Preheat the oven to 400°F (200°C).
2. In a small bowl, whisk together the Dijon mustard, olive oil, honey, thyme, salt, and pepper.
3. Rub the mustard mixture evenly over the chicken thighs.
4. Place the chicken thighs on a baking sheet and arrange lemon slices around them.
5. Roast for 35-40 minutes, or until the chicken is fully cooked and the skin is crispy.
6. Serve with roasted vegetables or a side salad.

Mustard Coleslaw

Ingredients:

- 4 cups shredded cabbage
- 1 cup shredded carrots
- 1/2 cup mayonnaise
- 2 tablespoons Dijon mustard
- 1 tablespoon apple cider vinegar
- 1 teaspoon honey
- Salt and pepper to taste

Instructions:

1. In a large bowl, combine the shredded cabbage and carrots.
2. In a separate bowl, whisk together the mayonnaise, Dijon mustard, apple cider vinegar, honey, salt, and pepper.
3. Pour the dressing over the cabbage mixture and toss until evenly coated.
4. Chill in the refrigerator for at least 30 minutes before serving to allow the flavors to meld.

Mustard and Bacon Deviled Eggs

Ingredients:

- 6 hard-boiled eggs, halved
- 3 tablespoons mayonnaise
- 1 tablespoon Dijon mustard
- 1 teaspoon white wine vinegar
- 1 teaspoon honey
- 2 strips of bacon, cooked and crumbled
- Salt and pepper to taste
- Paprika for garnish

Instructions:

1. Remove the yolks from the halved eggs and place them in a bowl.
2. Mash the yolks with a fork, then add mayonnaise, Dijon mustard, white wine vinegar, honey, salt, and pepper. Stir until smooth.
3. Spoon or pipe the yolk mixture back into the egg whites.
4. Top with crumbled bacon and a sprinkle of paprika.
5. Chill before serving.

Mustard-Crusted Roasted Lamb

Ingredients:

- 1 rack of lamb (about 1.5 lbs)
- 3 tablespoons Dijon mustard
- 2 cloves garlic, minced
- 1 tablespoon fresh rosemary, chopped
- 1 tablespoon olive oil
- Salt and pepper to taste

Instructions:

1. Preheat the oven to 400°F (200°C).
2. In a small bowl, mix together Dijon mustard, minced garlic, rosemary, olive oil, salt, and pepper.
3. Rub the mustard mixture all over the rack of lamb.
4. Place the lamb on a roasting pan and roast for 25-30 minutes, or until the internal temperature reaches 135°F (57°C) for medium-rare.
5. Let the lamb rest for 5-10 minutes before slicing and serving.

www.ingramcontent.com/pod-product-compliance
Lightning Source LLC
LaVergne TN
LVHW061955070526
838199LV00060B/4141